Original title:
The Roof Over My Heart

Copyright © 2025 Creative Arts Management OÜ
All rights reserved.

Author: Ronan Whitfield
ISBN HARDBACK: 978-1-80587-076-0
ISBN PAPERBACK: 978-1-80587-546-8

Heartbeats Beneath Covering Stars

Under the cover, we snugly lie,
Whispers of dreams as the night flies by.
With pillows of laughter, we float away,
Counting the giggles till the break of day.

The moon eavesdrops on our silly chats,
While the cat auditioned for a role as a brat.
Your pillow fights always start the brawl,
Yet here I am, loving it all.

Blankets like clouds, we drift and dive,
In our own world, where we thrive.
Shouting at shadows that dance on the wall,
We've built a fortress, the tallest of all.

In the chill of night, we bundle tight,
Sharing our snacks and the last bit of bite.
Your snore is a symphony I can't resist,
In this cozy chaos, it's love that persists.

Clarity Between Constellations

In a world of twinkling lights,
I've lost my car keys twice!
A map to the stars, or just my dreams?
Navigating love with pizza slices.

The Hidden Chamber of Reflection

I gaze in the mirror, what do I see?
A classic dilemma of laundry and tea.
The hair and the socks in a cosmic dance,
Shows love's power in every glance.

Under the Canopy of Time

Underneath the clocks that tick,
I juggle my snacks, it's quite a trick.
Time laughs loudly, hands up in air,
While I trip over love like a clown in despair.

Love's Shield of Stars

With a cape made of wishes, I dash to impress,
But trip on my shoelace, oh what a mess!
The stars chuckle softly, their twinkle so bright,
In love's silly dance, I'll find my delight.

Curtain of Tenderness

When life throws pies and cream,
I just laugh and join the scheme.
With a splash of joy, we play,
Making messes every day.

A shield of laughter, bright and bold,
In our cozy nook, we're gold.
Through the ups and silly downs,
We wear our crazy like crowns.

Encased in a Gentle Embrace

Hugs that squish like doughy bread,
Tickles dancing on your head.
In this warmth, I'm safe and sound,
With you, silly glee abounds.

Our clumsy waltz, two left feet,
Makes each moment so complete.
Cartwheels through the living room,
Brighten up the dullest gloom.

Beneath the Umbrella of Us

Raindrops plop, what a funny sight,
Together we jump, hearts so light.
With every splash, we sing our tune,
Underneath the laughing moon.

Dancing puddles in the street,
Searching for the next sweet treat.
In this bubble of delight,
Even storms feel just right.

Enclosed in Warmth

In our blanket fort, we hide,
Where giggles and snacks collide.
With silly stories and loud cheers,
We chase away all grown-up fears.

A throne of pillows, soft and round,
In this kingdom, love is found.
With every jellybean we share,
Life's a joke, and we don't care.

The Vaulted Stars Above

Beneath a sky with winks so bright,
Laughter bubbles like soda with a bite.
We dance like raindrops on a tin roof,
In this humor-filled space, we find our proof.

A squirrel in a hat tips his furry brow,
As we share dreams that somehow seem to wow.
Bouncing like beans in a fun-filled jar,
We're silly, we're crazy, our hearts are bizarre.

The Gables of Togetherness

Under the eaves, we find our cheer,
With jokes that tickle and tug at our ear.
The ceiling might sag with our endless fun,
But we'll keep laughing till the day is done.

Our kitchen's a circus; the sink is a stage,
With each clattering dish, we unleash our rage.
From pies that flop to soufflés that fall,
In this tangled chaos, we still have a ball.

Echoes of Laughter Around Us

Echoes bounce off the walls with glee,
As we chase the cat who's not quite so free.
She leaps like a rocket when we bring the treats,
Her antics are more than just silly feats.

The tickle of a feather, a snap of a cap,
Each moment's a treasure, a chuckle, a clap.
With whispers of joy in our little abode,
We pile up the joys, like a jigsaw code.

Textures of Home

Cushions are castles, tables are plains,
With playful banter, we dance through the chains.
Each spot tells a story, each crack's a delight,
Like an old-timey film, it's our secret light.

We've got socks that wander and shoes that will sway,
In a ballet of chaos, they twist and they play.
Oh, what a mess, yet we laugh through it all,
In this cozy habitat, we'll never let fall.

Whispers Wrapped in Tenderness

In the attic of giggles, we play,
Chasing shadows like kids in the fray.
With secret snacks hidden high in the air,
We laugh 'til we tumble, lose all our care.

Tickles from whispers float softly about,
Each silly joke ends with a loud shout.
Pillows our fortress, giggles our shield,
In this warm castle, no joy is concealed.

The Foundation of Togetherness

We built our love out of laughter and mess,
With socks on the ceiling, it's quite a success.
The kitchen's a canvas, we paint with delight,
Spaghetti on walls is our favorite sight.

In our fort of old blankets, we scheme and we dream,
Plotting adventures fueled by ice cream.
With each silly moment, we strengthen the base,
A zany foundation with smiles we embrace.

Beneath the Glistening Ceilings

Under twinkling lights, we dance like the fool,
Our spaghetti dance moves should earn us a school.
With cupfuls of giggles spilling on the floor,
We'll serenade squirrels outside by the door.

Each ceiling a canvas for dreams and delight,
We paint our chaos, making wrongs into right.
Trusting the humor to see us through each,
Surrounded by laughter, nothing's out of reach.

Shades of Warmth and Grace

In comfy pajamas, we host a grand show,
With our couch as the stage, don't steal the flow.
The dog is the star, with a bow of pure fluff,
As we laugh at his antics, we can't get enough.

With blankets as capes, we save the day bright,
Armed with our tickles, we conquer the night.
In silly adventures, we find our embrace,
United in laughter, our favorite place.

The Archway of Affection

Underneath the arch, we laugh and play,
Our silly antics brighten the day.
With a wink and a grin, we dance with glee,
Who knew love could be so funny, you see?

Beneath this structure, our jokes collide,
Like two goofy fools with nothing to hide.
Tickles and giggles, what a delight,
Every shared chuckle feels perfectly right.

Nestled in Sentiment

In cozy nooks, we snicker and tease,
Spilling secrets like leaves from the trees.
Whispers of warmth in a playful tone,
Together we craft a world of our own.

With pillows as shields, we duel with flair,
I throw a soft one, but you're never there.
Jumping the couch for a comical chase,
Our nest of sentiment, a funny place.

A Fortress of Feelings

Built from laughter, our walls stand tall,
Echoes of jokes fill this fortress hall.
With every punchline, our spirits soar,
In this comfy kingdom, who could want more?

We guard our treasures, with giggles and shouts,
Deflecting the worries that life brings about.
On the battlements, we strike a pose,
With silly faces, our affection shows.

The Enclosure of Love

Within this space, the fun never stops,
We bounce off each other, like bumps and hops.
Chasing the shadows, we tease and poke,
In our little bubble, laughter's no joke.

With every shared glance, humor ignites,
Cracking up over silly life fights.
In this enclosure, we always find bliss,
A hearty chuckle, our sweetest kiss.

Quiet Courtyards of the Heart

In my mind's garden, there's a play,
Where giggles bloom and chase decay.
A squirrel's running with my socks,
While I'm outsmarted by feathered flocks.

In quiet corners, laughter leaks,
As shadows dance, my spirit speaks.
A cat's had tea with my old shoes,
Whiskers twitching, sharing the news.

Rain taps soft on the window frame,
Each drop a pet that's lost its name.
Whimsy weaves through every sight,
In these courtyards, hearts take flight.

The Vault of My Sentiments

In this vault, emotions mill,
Where silly jars are filled with thrill.
I find a hat from days gone by,
It tells me all the reasons why.

A treasure trove of mismatched socks,
And silly notes in crumbling blocks.
Each piece a giggle, no need for shame,
As I relive those awkward games.

The locks may rust, the doors may creak,
But here's the spot where laughter peaks.
In this vault, joy's a priceless art,
Filled to the brim, a quirky heart.

Anchored by Love's Light

A lighthouse stands where shadows play,
Guiding my boats in a comical way.
With each wave, a well-timed quirk,
Sails flapping like a chicken's jerk.

Through stormy skies and calm, sweet nights,
My heart's compass finds its sights.
A beam that winks, a glow so bright,
Makes even thunder giggle with fright.

With love as anchor, I can't drift far,
Every journey brings a smile, a scar.
In this harbor, joy is the plight,
Sailing through storms with pure delight.

Blossoms in the Attic

In dusty corners, secrets bloom,
Old toys giggle, spreading their gloom.
A rubber chicken's made a nest,
With tattered tales that never rest.

A sunflower sprouting from an old shoe,
Sings rock'n'roll to a paper crew.
The attic's warmth holds silly dreams,
While laughter whispers through the seams.

Bright colors clash in splendid chaos,
With memories peeking just to play boss.
Among the branches, joy does sprout,
In every petal, laughter's about.

Under the Eaves of Togetherness

Under laughing shingles we chuckle,
With coffee spills and playful muckle.
Beneath the rain, we dance and sway,
In our cozy nook, we jest each day.

Squirrels drop nuts, plan a heist,
While we munch on snacks—what a feast!
Though storms may rage, we gleefully grin,
In our own silliness, true joy begins.

Hearth of Hope and Warmth

The fire crackles, more jokes than heat,
From marshmallows burnt to burnt feet.
We share our dreams, some wild and absurd,
And ponder the meaning of that one weird bird.

Chairs wobble, laughter fills the air,
With socks mismatched, beyond compare.
Our worries fade like smoke up high,
As giggles echo, and time flies by.

Arc of Emotions

We swing through moods like on a vine,
From melodrama to cheese and wine.
With each twist, the view's a riot,
Our grins grow wide, as we start a quiet.

Sometimes we're serious, it's hard to believe,
Yet a wink or a hiccup makes us weave.
Through madness and giggles, hand in hand,
Together we thrive, a carefree band.

The Lantern's Glow in the Quiet Night

Beneath the glow, shadows play tricks,
Making ghosts of our whims, they flick.
We share secret stories and conspiracies,
That make us snort and roll, oh the eeries!

As we munch on snacks—crunch, chew, and sigh,
The night winks back, oh my, oh my!
With eyes that twinkle, tales are spun,
In the lantern's glow, our laughter runs.

Treasures Stored in the Attic of Hope

In the attic where dreams lie,
A cat wearing glasses asks why.
Old toys reminiscing their cheer,
Dance dust devils, never fear.

A hat that once flew on a kite,
Whispers tales of silly delight.
Amidst cobwebs and squeaks so bright,
Hope sways like a feather in flight.

The Kiss of Protection

Beneath a roof made of giggles,
I found marshmallows that wiggle.
Better than any shield, oh dear,
Laughter wraps me, draws me near.

With every chuckle, skies align,
A fortress built with punchlines,
Each snort and waddle, a warm embrace,
Funny faces fill this space.

Wrapped in a Gossamer Veil

Wrapped in laughter, soft as mist,
Where clowns and puppies coexist.
Tickles dance, like butterflies,
Under a canopy of sighs.

A veil spun from whimsy's thread,
Hides all worries, fears, and dread.
As giggles float like balloons on high,
Joy's the reason we reach for the sky.

Serenity in the Dome of Affection

In a dome where hugs play peek,
We chase our shadows, hide and seek.
With fluffiest pillows, we convene,
Laughing 'til we turn green.

Here, even grumpy cats can cheer,
With purring jokes that we all hear.
In love's warm arms, a gentle jest,
Happiness blooms, we're truly blessed.

Brimming with Comfort

In a house where laughter rings,
Cats and dogs play silly games.
Socks become the latest trend,
And I can't find the blame!

Cereal spills like morning rain,
I dance in puddles of cheer.
Nothing beats this silly mess,
With chocolate milk and good beer.

The fridge hums songs of delight,
As leftovers scream, "Eat me now!"
Neighbors peek in with big eyes wide,
Like they just saw a cow!

Comfort's in the chaos loud,
In every giggle and mishap.
It's here I find my happy place,
In laughter, hugs, and a nap.

The Sky Within Four Walls

A ceiling painted blue and bright,
Holds dreams that wander high.
Clouds drift in from the old fan's spin,
While I sip tea and sigh.

Pillows stacked like little hills,
Form peaks of comfy bliss.
I climb them daily just for kicks,
And wish my chores were amiss.

Windows framed with silliness,
Birds take notes on my dance.
They chirp as if they're laughing loud,
At my own silly prance!

Sunlight spills in like a joke,
And shadows play a silly game.
Here in my tiny sky of peace,
Every day feels the same.

A Sanctuary of Sentiments

Each corner tells a funny tale,
Of socks lost in the couch's depths.
Memories on the fridge's door,
With magnets securing my breaths.

A chair that squeaks and moans so loud,
It joins me for some tea.
We laugh together, both of us,
What's better than company?

Walls adorned with crayon art,
From kids who made a mess.
Every scribble holds a giggle,
In my cozy, heartfelt nest.

Time ticks by with playful grace,
Warmth fills the air with cheer.
In this sanctuary of mine,
I find joy, love, and beer!

Whispered Secrets in Shelter

Underneath a blanket fort,
We plot against the world outside.
Pillow fights and squeaky toys,
Here laughter cannot hide.

Secrets shared in hushed delight,
As popcorn falls like rain.
Stories twist and turn with glee,
Spinning tales of joy and pain.

Walls may echo with our fun,
As feet dance to happy tunes.
In this place of lovely chaos,
We're closer than the moon!

Every whisper, every giggle,
Keeps our spirits soaring high.
In this shelter made with love,
We wave our worries goodbye.

A Fort of Memories

In the backyard, we built a dream,
Old sheets and chairs, a wild theme.
Teddy bears stood as sentinels,
Guarding giggles and silly spells.

Underneath, we shared our snacks,
Mismatched socks and silly hacks.
Fortress of laughter, joy unfurled,
In this bubble, we ruled the world.

Time moved slow, we'd tell tall tales,
Counting clouds and happy trails.
With flashlights casting spooky sights,
We'd conquer fears on those starry nights.

When the storm clouds laughed and played,
We'd sing our songs and not be swayed.
In our fort, nothing could break through,
Just a world of me and you.

Wings of Comfort Above

On sunny days, we'd fly so high,
With bedsheets draped across the sky.
Imaginary friends took flight,
As we soared towards the shining light.

Banana boats and chocolate pies,
Launching dreams that spark and rise.
Each flap of wings, a silly cheer,
As we left all our doubt and fear.

Rainy days brought paper planes,
With laundry lines as our new lanes.
We'd race the clouds, so soft and slow,
Laughing at where the puddles go.

Nestled close, we'd dream and plot,
Creating worlds in our backyard spot.
No heights too great, we would explore,
With laughter echoing forevermore.

The Fortress of Togetherness

In the living room, we stacked those chairs,
Creating walls that caught our glares.
Cushion turrets, blankets galore,
Defending joy from the mundane chore.

Every corner held a secret laugh,
As we created our own path.
Inside these walls, the world stood still,
Surrounded by warmth, a magic thrill.

With a cardboard sword and a funny hat,
We brought the knights and dragons flat.
Fending off the tickle fights,
In this kingdom, we claimed our rights.

When afternoon sun turned to night,
Fairy tales filled the dimming light.
Side by side, we made a pact,
In this fortress, joy is intact.

Canopy of Kindred Souls

Under the branches, we'd find our place,
With laughter echoing, a wild chase.
Swinging from roots, we danced and played,
A canopy where fears allayed.

Beneath, we made our secret plans,
With peanut butter and jelly sandwiches in hands.
Telling tales of dragons and knights,
Every word sparked magical flights.

As twilight fell, we'd share our dreams,
Plotting journeys down sparkling streams.
The stars listened with twinkling eyes,
In this shelter, imagination flies.

A canopy woven with threads of fun,
With silly voices and races run.
Together we'd laugh, and together we'd sing,
In this patch of joy, life's sweetest spring.

When Coverings Embrace

In a world so wide and vast,
I found a spot that holds me fast.
Where laughter echoes off the walls,
And silliness always calls.

The ceiling's low, the jokes are high,
With goofy hats made from the sky.
Every beam a friend you'll find,
In this cozy space, we're intertwined.

The comfort here is thick as cheese,
We'll sip on tea and bite on peas.
With pillows stacked and tales to spin,
We'll giggle loud, let the fun begin.

So here's to laughter, joy, and play,
In our quirky haven, we'll always stay.
With love that wraps like a warm cocoon,
We dance and sing, a delightful tune.

The Haven of Unspoken Words

In this place, words can be shy,
But oh, the laughter flits and flies!
A glance, a wink, that says it all,
Underneath the laughter's gall.

The corners hide a playful tease,
Where mismatched socks become the breeze.
Our secrets swirl in silent flight,
In this haven, the world feels right.

A shoe on the ceiling, a cat with glee,
Who knew love looked funny? Just wait and see.
We share our snacks and goofy dreams,
In this refuge of giggles and beams.

With every chuckle, the walls grow bright,
We spin our tales into the night.
Unspoken bonds in joyful bursts,
In this haven, our hearts quench their thirst.

A Shield of Affection

When the world outside feels ill at ease,
We find our joy in awkward tease.
With blanket forts and cookies stacked,
Our playful hearts are now intact.

The walls are thick with love and glee,
With every mishap, it's you and me.
A sprinkling of socks, a dash of flair,
A shield of smiles is always there.

When belly laughs take over the night,
We create our own delight and light.
In this fortress where the silly reigns,
Affection flows through our silly veins.

So raise a toast to love so sweet,
In our own space, feel the fun repeat.
We'll conquer the gloom with our charming quirks,
In a shield of joy, where laughter lurks.

Under the Eaves of Connection

Beneath the eaves where laughter lives,
We trade our secrets, and joy it gives.
With every chuckle, a bond we weave,
In this embrace, we never leave.

A shelf of toys, a cat that snores,
Here, silliness always restores.
Our heartbeats echo with every joke,
In this sweet nook, where fun awoke.

We sip on laughter, we snack on cheer,
With quirky dances, we draw near.
In silly hats and mismatched shoes,
We find the spark that we could choose.

So, under this roof of tales and glee,
We forge connections, you and me.
In this haven of joy, we're forever entwined,
Under the eaves, our hearts aligned.

A Canopy of Love

In my garden, weeds sprout tall,
But love's warmth makes me feel small.
With laughter, we dance, side by side,
Umbrellas up, in joy we hide.

Sipping tea in goofy hats,
We make up jokes like silly cats.
Underneath our colorful shade,
The funny moments never fade.

A pillow fight with pillows soft,
We giggle loud, our spirits loft.
Like squirrels chasing a wanderer's cheer,
In this canopy, nothing to fear.

So lift your tea and toast to cheer,
For love and laughter are always near.
With silly grins and clumsy moves,
In this warm space, our joy improves.

Between the Beams of Affection

Building dreams with wobbly beams,
We laugh at life, or so it seems.
With each plank placed, we share a grin,
Companions in mischief, let's begin!

Dancing this quirky jig, my friend,
Our laughter's bricks, they never bend.
We trip on love, then smile wide,
Navigating life with love as our guide.

Between the beams, we poke fun,
Guessing who might get hit by the sun.
From spilled tea to soft shoe slips,
We find humor in our mishaps' trips.

So hold on tight, for here we go,
With squeaky laughter in tow.
Together, we build, with care and jest,
In our silly shack, we are truly blessed.

The Safe Harbor of Emotion

In this harbor, boats sway indeed,
But my heart's an anchor, a sturdy seed.
We toss jokes like rope and sail,
Navigating storms with our holy grail.

With fishy puns and dolphin dives,
We anchor down where laughter thrives.
Though waves may crash and tempests call,
Our giggles do reign supreme through all.

Under stars, we share our dreams,
With slippery jokes and marshmallow creams.
Building castles on sandy shores,
In our laughter, the ocean roars.

So here we drift, through joy and strife,
In this harbor, we find our life.
With a wink and a laugh, we'll never part,
For this ocean flows deep in our heart.

Under the Cover of Solitude

In the blanket fort of my quiet space,
I giggle at shadows that race.
With snacks piled high and movies too,
My solitude sings a quirky tune.

Socks mismatched and hair a frizz,
I'm a chaotic creature of sheer bliss.
Every pillow whispers a secret or two,
In laughter's embrace, the world feels new.

Flipping popcorn like it's a sport,
I chuckle alone, never to be caught.
Witty thoughts in my brain do stew,
Creating laughter for me and you.

So here I stay, in my cozy cocoon,
With giggles and dreams, I'm over the moon.
In this merry home of solitude,
I find joy's dance in a lighthearted mood.

Thatch of Trust

In a land of odd leaps and bounds,
Where laughter is found on the ground,
We built a space free of doubt,
With hugs that never run out.

A quirky home shaped like a shoe,
Where socks dance and giggles ensue,
The walls made of marshmallows too,
We toast to the funny things we do.

Through doors that squeak like a song,
We cherish each moment, never wrong,
With banter that bounces, bright and loud,
In a silly kingdom, we're ever proud.

So here's to the slanted roof we share,
With mischief and mayhem filling the air,
In laughter we find our common ground,
Where joy is the treasure we have found.

The Embrace of a Familiar Sky

Beneath a ceiling of bright blue cheer,
Where clouds giggle and squirrels appear,
We dance like no one's watching us,
In our cozy nook, no need to fuss.

With words that twirl like dandelion seeds,
We share our hopes and quirky deeds,
Each glance a spark, each smile a grin,
In this space, we let the fun begin.

The stars at night throw winks so sly,
As we sip our tea with a perplexed sigh,
Our hearts take flight on balloons of fate,
In the sweetest spot, we celebrate!

So let the moonlight tickle our feet,
And make our laughter echo and repeat,
In this charming sky, we find our place,
Where joy and silliness leave a trace.

Sunbeams and Shadows Intertwined

In a sunbeam's kiss, we take our stance,
With shadows that giggle and dance,
Our ticklish toes meet the floor,
As silly moments beg for more.

Like puzzle pieces, unwittingly wed,
With playful antics that flood our bed,
We race around corners, no time to waste,
In this cat-and-mouse of joy embraced.

The sun throws rays, the shadows play tricks,
As we tumble through laughter, a bag of quick fixes,
A trampoline made of our silly dreams,
Launching us high on whimsical streams.

So let's soar up high, take flight anew,
In a circus of giggles, just me and you,
With beams and shadows, forever entwined,
In this humorous journey, joy's always defined.

The Bridge of Understanding

Between us lies a bridge of fun,
Where silly faces cause chaos to run,
With each step, we wobble and sway,
Laughing aloud at the games we play.

Through laughter's language and giggling signs,
We navigate feelings, like twirling vines,
With puns that pop and jokes like fireflies,
Creating delight in our joyful eyes.

Like frogs on lily pads, we leap and croak,
Riffing off puns that make us joke,
Our bridge is sturdy, built on respect,
With every chuckle, we connect.

So here's to the path we choose to tread,
With whimsical thoughts swirling in our head,
In this funny realm where we share our spark,
Building bridges that light up the dark.

A Refuge from the World

When life gets tough, I hide away,
In my cozy nook, I choose to stay.
A fortress built of snacks and sighs,
Where giggles triumph, and worry flies.

Popcorn clouds and chocolate streams,
Reality melts into silly dreams.
My pets become the kings and queens,
In this domain of goofy scenes.

Outside's a mess, but in here, it's fun,
With pillow fights, we've already won.
The world can wait; I'm here to play,
In my fortress, it's a holiday.

So if you're lost, just come on by,
We'll build a fort and watch time fly.
With laughter echoing, we'll find a way,
In this refuge where we'll always stay.

The Umbrella of Affection

When raindrops fall, we take our stand,
Beneath a bright and polka-dot brand.
You laugh and twirl, I start to spin,
Under this shade, let the fun begin.

The world gets wet, but we stay dry,
With every splash, our spirits fly.
A dance of joy, a waltz for two,
Under our cover, it's just me and you.

Huddled close, we share a snack,
A soggy sandwich, but that's a fact.
Giggles roll like thunderclaps,
Together in the silly mishaps.

So let it pour; we're warm inside,
With umbrella bright, there's no need to hide.
Through puddles big, we'll bounce and glide,
In this swirling storm, we're on a joyride.

Shelter in Moments of Silence

In corners quiet, we share a glance,
Amidst the chaos, we take a chance.
A whisper here, a snort of glee,
In our secret bubble, just you and me.

The world outside can bark and howl,
But in our silence, we laugh and growl.
Potato chips crunch, loud as a drum,
As we savor our peace, it's blissful and numb.

Let others shout, we find a way,
In silence thick, we joyfully play.
Your silly face, a priceless gem,
In these quiet moments, the bliss begins.

So snuggle close, let the quiet rest,
In the pause of laughter, we feel so blessed.
In our little world, it's easy to see,
Silence is fun, with you next to me.

The Harmonious Arch of Us

Together we create a silly show,
With mismatched socks and a funny glow.
A duet of jokes, in perfect sync,
As harmony brews with every wink.

We dance through life, a two-headed beast,
With laughter flowing, we never cease.
Your puns hit hard, like pies in the face,
In this arch of giggles, we find our place.

Sometimes we clash, in a playful way,
Like cats and dogs, we frolic and play.
Yet no matter the squabble, we know deep down,
In our funny kingdom, there's never a frown.

So join me here, in this joyful ride,
Under the arch where our quirks collide.
With you by my side, there's always a fuss,
In this laughter-filled dome, the best kind of us.

Sheltering Emotions

Underneath my quirky hat,
Lies a heart that loves to chat.
It shelters giggles day and night,
With corny jokes that feel just right.

Beneath this canopy of cheer,
Worries vanish, not a tear.
With puns and laughter, I'm secure,
In my home where joy's the cure.

Each ticklish breeze, each funny pun,
Makes life feel like a dash of fun.
With wobbly chairs and playful cats,
My shelter's full of love like that.

So here I stand, all snug and neat,
In my cozy corner, life's a treat.
With every smile and playful glance,
I dance beneath this heart-shaped trance.

Beneath the Canopy of Care

Underneath this quirky tree,
Love's odd branches dance with glee.
With leaves of laughter, roots of cheer,
I find my shelter, always near.

Beneath this canopy so bright,
Worries fade into the night.
Where tickles grow, and puns are shared,
In this warm space, no one's scared.

With squirrels cracking jokes up high,
And playful shadows fluttering by,
Each moment brings a funny spree,
As love's secure as it can be.

In this delightful, joyful glade,
All fears dissolve; they're softly laid.
With laughter ringing everywhere,
I know I'm safe, beneath this care.

Love's Protective Arch

Beneath the arch of silly dreams,
Where love flows like ice cream streams.
With whipped cream smiles and cherry cheer,
This archway holds us, always near.

Giggles echo in this space,
Every moment filled with grace.
With wobbly steps and dance moves bold,
Our love's a story, brightly told.

Overhead, a laughter sun,
Keeps us warm, and oh so fun.
With playful jests and gentle nudges,
Every day a joy that budges.

So here we stay, forever spry,
Beneath this arch, we aim for the sky.
With silly hats and friendly glances,
Love's protective arch enhances.

Hearts Beneath a Starlit Dome

Beneath this sky, so wide and bright,
Our hearts embrace the sheer delight.
With twinkling stars, and laughter's tune,
We find our joy, beneath the moon.

Silly jokes dance in the air,
Like fireflies, with not a care.
Each giggle's spark, a starry show,
All worries vanish, soft and slow.

In cuddled warmth, we share and play,
With playful hearts that light the way.
This starlit dome, our cheerful home,
It welcomes all, no need to roam.

So side by side, we dream and scheme,
In this vast sky, life feels like a dream.
With every chuckle, every sigh,
Beneath these stars, we aim to fly.

Cradle of Kindness

In a house made of giggles, we dance,
Where socks keep their secrets, like a fine romance.
The walls hold our laughter, they wear a grin,
As cookies crash parties, let the fun begin!

Beneath the chandelier of crumbs and cheer,
We waltz with the dust bunnies, they know no fear.
In every corner, a tale does reside,
With mischief and mayhem, we take it in stride.

The cushions are pillows of dreams yet to soar,
Where slumbers become replays of pranks and rapport.
With every twist and turn, joy takes its place,
An abode of oddities, love's funny embrace.

So here's to the chaos that fills every day,
To the brilliant nonsense that leads us astray.
In the cradle of kindness, we find our groove,
Where life's little quirks are the ultimate move.

Structure of Tender Moments

In a house of wild wonders, we build with delight,
Foam swords serving justice, all through the night.
Laughter erupts like popcorn in air,
As we harness our whims with mischievous flair.

Blueprints in crayon map life's silly quest,
Each room is a playground where joy feels blessed.
Wobbly tables hold secrets of tea,
Where sippy cups overflow with glee.

Windows of whimsy let sunshine in,
As we juggle our chores with a laugh and a spin.
The hallways echo stories we share,
With sock puppets chatting, they never despair.

Oh, the foundation of warmth that we share,
With a sprinkle of chaos and a dash of flair.
Here in this structure, our hearts intertwine,
Where moments are tender, yet oh-so-divine!

The Overhang of Memory

Under the eaves where the memories cling,
We trip over laughter, oh what a fling!
Dust bunnies waltz while the dishes debate,
And shoes on the porch play a game of their fate.

The attic holds treasures of old silly times,
With hats made of giggles and old nursery rhymes.
Drawing maps on the walls with a crayon flair,
A treasure hunt waits for those willing to dare.

We dangle our hopes from the rafters so high,
While whispers of joy float up to the sky.
Each shadow a story, each echo a song,
In the overhang of memories, we fatefully belong.

So let's raise a toast with our mismatched cups,
To the tales that unite us and fill us with ups.
In the corners of kindness, let giggles take hold,
For these are the stories that never grow old.

Shielding My Heart's Reverie

In a kingdom of cushions, where dreams take flight,
Pajama-clad warriors prepare for a fight.
With pizza box shields and candy-bar swords,
We laugh at the battles and joy in the hoards.

The fortress we build, with popcorn and cheer,
Is a safe haven where all feel near.
While crayon winds swirl, stories come alive,
In this fortress of fun, our spirits thrive.

Beneath the canopy of mismatched decor,
We gather together, we echo with more.
Each giggle and guffaw creates a new lane,
Shielding our hearts, where love's never plain.

So let us rejoice in this place that we make,
With marshmallow dreams and a big slice of cake.
In this realm of delight, forever we'll stay,
For laughter's our language, in every way.

The Overhang of Trust

When the rain falls soft, I smile,
For your umbrella is wide and style.
The secrets we share, under this dome,
Even squirrels think it's a lovely home.

Together we laugh, while storms do play,
A bit of your madness keeps worries at bay.
In puddles we jump, mud splatters fly,
With you by my side, I can almost fly!

Trust is a dance on slippery ground,
With you, my dear, I've truly found.
An overhang that giggles with grace,
In this goofy space, I've found my place.

So bring on the thunder, let lightning spark,
We'll just build a fort, right here in the dark.
With laughter to shield us, we'll weather it all,
Under our canvas, I will never fall.

Embracing Shadows and Light

In the dimmest of corners, we play peek-a-boo,
Making shadows wiggle, just me and you.
Your jokes are like sunshine, bright and spry,
As we dance 'round the dark, oh me, oh my!

Caught in a giggle, with laughter we play,
Bouncing off walls in a silly ballet.
You're the sparkle in gloom, my playful knight,
With you in the haze, all's perfectly right.

Two clowns in a circus, out on a spree,
Riding the carousel, just you and me.
We gather light like it's confetti,
In the shadows we hug, both warm and petty.

So let's twirl through the twilight, a grand parade,
With mismatched socks, all colorful and frayed.
You bring the laughter, I'll fetch the delight,
Together we shine, embracing the night.

The Covering of Kindred Spirits

Two peas in a pod, we're oddly aligned,
With quirks and with quirks, perfectly combined.
You snort when you laugh, oh, what a dear,
Next to you, my troubles just disappear.

Our blanket of love, a patchwork design,
With pockets of joy, both yours and mine.
We gather like cats on a sunbeam's end,
Life's silliness rises, a beautiful blend.

With wit as my armor, I'm ready for jest,
Your laughter my shield, I'm feeling quite blessed.
We conquer the mundane, each day a bright spree,
In our vibrant cocoon, we laugh wild and free.

So when life gets tricky, hold my hand tight,
In this cozy cocoon, everything's bright.
Together we thrive, two hearts on a quest,
In the covering of laughter, we're truly the best.

Armor of Affection

In a world that's a tangle, we suit up for fun,
Our armor's got glitter, and make-believe guns.
With heart-shaped shields and giggles galore,
We'll march through the mayhem, just wanting more.

Each poke and each jab brings laughter so wild,
You're my silly pal, forever my child.
With marshmallow swords, we battle quite sweet,
In a fortress of joy, no one can compete.

We dodge all the drama, trading jests like coins,
Dancing in pajamas, twirls in the joins.
The fabric of friendship, a quilt over time,
In this bonkers adventure, we're perfectly prime.

So raise up your glass, here's a toast to our team,
In the armor of laughter, we live on a dream.
Together we shine, through all ups and downs,
In this zany life, we wear our own crowns.

The Hearthstone of Hope

In the kitchen, we burn the toast,
Laughter erupts, we're quite the host.
With every spill, our spirits fly,
Dancing around, as smoke fills the sky.

The cat steals bites from our dinner,
While we race to see who's the winner.
Cooking chaos, it's quite the scene,
Yet love brews here, you know what I mean.

Jokes are cracked like eggs on the floor,
We trip, we slip, then shout for more.
A recipe made from silly sings,
In this cozy den, where joy always clings.

So raise a glass, to our little mess,
In this hearthstone, we're truly blessed.
With laughter bubbling in every heart,
In our loving kitchen, we play our part.

A Canopy of Untold Stories

Beneath this roof, where tales collide,
We share our dreams, with a wink and pride.
A sock on the puppy, oh what a sight,
Makes it hard to keep a straight face tonight.

The couch is a ship, we're pirates bold,
Every cushion, a treasure of stories untold.
We voyage through moments, with laughter afloat,
As the dog plays captain, in his silly coat.

Imagining monsters who dance at our feet,
The laughter echoes, a rhythmic beat.
With secrets and giggles, the hours fly,
In this canopy of fun, we reach for the sky.

So gather 'round, let the stories spin,
In this joyful place, we all fit in.
With every chuckle, our bonds will grow,
Under our roof, love's light will glow.

Cloaked in Resilience

When the rain drops tap like a silly song,
Our dancing socks say, "Come join along!"
With mud on the floor, we twirl with glee,
What chaos unfolds, but oh, what a spree!

Life's little hiccups, we turn to gold,
Like a clown at the circus, we're brave and bold.
With every mishap, we wear our grin,
In pajamas of joy, we know we can win.

So here we are, in this joyful mess,
Each tumble and stumble, we truly bless.
For in our hearts, resilience thrives,
As we gather our laughter, it drastically jives.

No matter the storms that come our way,
With smiles so bright, we're here to stay.
Cloaked in our humor, we stand so tall,
In this quirky abode, we conquer all.

Embraced by Serenity

In the quiet corners where whispers dwell,
Relaxed, we giggle like kids, oh so well.
With warm cups of cocoa, we settle in,
As each clumsy sip becomes a win.

The clock ticks softly, like a gentle hum,
Jokes about time make our brains go numb.
A delightful rebellion against the clock,
In this serene space, we lovingly mock.

Soothing laughter dances like fireflies,
In this gentle glow, the whacky lies.
With every chuckle, peace fills the air,
In this haven of joy, we cherish and share.

Here's to the moments that make us grin,
Fortified by love, we always win.
Embraced by calmness, in our silly retreat,
Together we flourish, oh, life is sweet!

The Loft of Longing

In a space where love may dwell,
I've got pizza, snack and gel.
My cats, they think they're kings up there,
As I trip over my old armchair.

Jokes echo off the crooked walls,
Echoing laughter, bouncing calls.
Socks are scattered, joy displayed,
In this haven, I've mislaid!

Last week it rained a funny tune,
While I hummed to the silver moon.
A dance with dust bunnies, we twirled,
As sticky notes just laughed and swirled.

Yet every corner holds a patch,
Of fluffy dreams in wild dispatch.
It's crammed but cozy, don't you see?
In this quirky penthouse, I'm wild and free.

Radiance Beneath the Ceiling

Underneath this dazzling light,
I wear my socks that never fight.
The broom laughs at my dust parade,
As I dance in my living-glade.

Awkward heights my thoughts might reach,
While my plants get all the speech.
They spill secrets with every spout,
While I proudly strut about.

My coffee spills, a friendly splash,
As I bounce in joy, make a dash.
There's laughter in the cans and jars,
While I play with misfit guitars.

Under this roof, I feel alive,
In a world where giggles thrive.
I may not have a grand parade,
But my happiness will never fade.

A Nest of Infinite Care

Inside this nest, my heart feels bold,
With secret snacks and stories told.
Cushioned laughter, piled high,
Throws and pillows reach the sky.

My old dog snores a gentle beat,
While I bring him snacks, a tasty treat.
We giggle at the chaos around,
In this realm of joy, I am crowned.

If walls could laugh, they'd know my fears,
But they choose giggles over tears.
Each mark a tale, each scrape a song,
In this haven, I belong.

In plush embraces, worries melt,
In this corner, warmth is felt.
It's a circus where my heart finds grace,
A smile rests on each funny face.

The Shield of Kindred Spirits

Under this arch of quirky flair,
My friends and I make quite the pair.
We trade our dreams, our pasta, too,
As laughter bubbles like morning dew.

We wear our mismatched socks with pride,
In this fortress, the giggles collide.
Patience tested like soft,
melting clay,
Through silly pranks, we seize the day.

Spills and thrills, we always cheer,
To celebrate each little year.
A pillow fort as headquarters,
In our world, there are no borders.

So here's to quirks and goofy styles,
In this sanctuary with endless smiles.
With every toast, we lift our hearts,
In this castle where the laughter starts.

Haven of Heartbeats

In a house of giggles, we dance and sway,
The cat tries to join, in its own silly way.
We bounce off the walls, fine art on display,
In laughter we paint, an all-night buffet.

With socks on our heads, we declare it a trend,
Each tickle and tease, my best little friend.
The kitchen's a mess, but we just won't bend,
These joyful escapades, they'll never end.

The fridge is a treasure, its contents so bright,
We feast on old pizza, who needs fine dining, right?
With pudding as currency, we barter in delight,
In our charming haven, we snicker and bite.

So here's to the chaos that makes our hearts sing,
With every wild moment, what fun we can bring.
In our playful sweet world, there's always a fling,
In the haven we built, joy's the ruling king.

The Archway of Belonging

Under a doorway, we'll shout and we'll cheer,
My goofy pals gather, bringing up the rear.
We joke 'bout the snacks, and which one is dear,
In this archway of joy, nothing to fear.

With pizza slice hats, we wear them with pride,
Creating new fables, where silliness slides.
Through portals of laughter, we wave and we glide,
In this magical space, all worries subside.

A jumble of blankets becomes our great throne,
A kingdom of giggles, where we're never alone.
With cookies for crowns, we sit on our own,
In this archway of belonging, we've all brightly shone.

So lift up a toast, to this odd little crew,
Where every strange moment is shining and new.
Our laughter, a bond, like old glue just won't strew,
In the archway of life, let's make our debut!

Whispers Beneath the Stars

Under the night sky, we lie very low,
With twinkling eyes, we put on our show.
We make up wild stories about all those glow,
Each star a secret, a story we sow.

There's a comet named Larry, who dances around,
His moves are so wacky, they can't make a sound.
Through cosmic confetti, our laughter is found,
In the whispers of night, our joy is unbound.

We count all the wishes, and giggle with glee,
As the moon draws closer, we all rearrange.
With marshmallows roasting, life's never a spree,
But beneath those stars, everything feels strange.

So here's to the night with its big sugary map,
To friends and good fortune, let's fill in the gap.
Our whispers, they flutter, as we giggle and clap,
In the cosmos of wonder, love's the great trap.

Shelter from the Storm

When raindrops come crashing, we snuggle up tight,
With popcorn and blankets, we vanish from sight.
The wind is a prankster, playing its flight,
But here in our fortress, we'll banish the fright.

With giggles and whispers, the shadows all creep,
Our fortress of fun, it's where we can leap.
We build our own castles, where secrets we keep,
In the heart of this storm, our joy runs so deep.

As puddles form lakes, we'll fashion a game,
With rubber duck races, all looking the same.
Each splash of adventure, we'll never blame,
For laughter and puddles, all part of the fame.

So bring on the thunder, let echoes unfold,
In this shelter of laughter, we'll break from the mold.
With warm hearts and smiles, we're never too old,
For rain is just comedy waiting to be told.

Sanctuary of Soulful Dreams

In a cozy nook where thoughts collide,
My mind's a circus, can't let it hide.
Laughter mingles with whispers and schemes,
Crafting a fortress from curious dreams.

Pillows piled high, a fort in the night,
Imaginary friends join in the delight.
Socks become banners, toast is a treat,
Who knew my refuge tasted so sweet?

Juggling my hopes like a clown on a wire,
Each thought a balloon, soaring higher and higher.
Chasing the giggles of shadows that play,
In my sanctuary, I dance through the day.

So let the world tremble, let it grow bold,
In this whimsical palace, no fear to behold.
With laughter as bricks, I build all around,
In this joyful haven, my heart is unbound.

Echoes in the Attic of My Mind

Up in the attic, where memories grin,
Hiding old treasures and laughter within.
Forgotten old toys start to conspire,
Whispering secrets of silly desires.

Dust bunnies dance to a tune so absurd,
As I stumble upon each misfit word.
Tickling my thoughts like a gentle breeze,
Echoes of chuckles brought down to their knees.

A mismatched chair crowned with old hats,
Winking at squirrels and friendly stray cats.
Maps of adventures drawn with no care,
Leading to places where nonsense is rare.

So I raise a glass to the attic so dear,
To stories and giggles that always appear.
In the echoes of whimsy, I find my way,
Where laughter unlocks all the mundane gray.

Beneath the Shelter of Your Smile

Under your smile, I find my place,
A patch of sun with a silly embrace.
Tickles of joy, a surprising start,
A fumble of laughter, a bright little spark.

Crooked little grins brighten the room,
Your giggles echo, dispelling the gloom.
We toss around jokes like a playful game,
Turning our mundane to wild and untame.

Beneath that smile, clouds drift away,
In our kingdom of chuckles, we frolic and play.
Silly stories shared, how the fun flows,
In this whimsical fortress, our laughter grows.

As we weave tales of banana peels,
Life's little mishaps become joy that heals.
So here's to the moments, both silly and mild,
Beneath that sweet smile, forever a child.

Layers of Protection and Passion

Wrapped in my layers, I'm snug as can be,
Woolen whims dissolve, like tea in the sea.
With scarves of laughter, I bundle my cheer,
Each thread a reminder that fun's always near.

Cardigans buttoned with stories untold,
Each flap like a tale, fit for the bold.
Fuzzy warm socks dance in delight,
As I twirl through the chaos, ignoring the night.

Bubble-wrap hearts in a world full of pranks,
Guarding our dreams with flexible flanks.
In a patchwork of giggles, we skip and we twirl,
Every moment a treasure in this whimsical whirl.

So let them unravel, let worries unspool,
Life's a grand canvas, and fun is the rule.
With layers of laughter and joy to protect,
We're wrapped in a love that we both can connect.

Bound by Warmth

In a cozy nook, we often sit,
With mismatched socks and endless wit.
A game of cards, who's the real champ?
Laughing so loud, we light up the lamp.

We argue over whose turn's it next,
With playful jabs, our banter perplexed.
Two bowls of popcorn, a movie begun,
We're trapped in our joy; who needs the sun?

From frozen pizzas to burnt toast,
We toast to the moments we cherish the most.
With every laugh, our worries take flight,
In this little space, everything feels right.

So here's to the warmth that we create,
In jumbled chaos, we spin our fate.
With humor as glue, we stick like tape,
In this silly love, there's always escape.

Embraced by the Night Sky

Under the stars, we pitch our tent,
Whispers of dreams and dreams that we sent.
S'mores melting into gooey delight,
We laugh at the shadows dancing in light.

A raccoon sneaks in for a snack or two,
We shoo it away, but it laughs back too!
With phantom sounds, we tell ghostly tales,
Daring each other, our courage unveils.

A blanket fort made from sheets and dreams,
Our living room fortress bursting at seams.
We play like kids, with hearts open wide,
In this cozy chaos, we take our pride.

So gaze at the sky, let your spirit soar,
With each twinkling star, we ask for more.
In this silly world, we're lost and found,
Embraced by laughter, forever spellbound.

A Haven for Heartstrings

In the small corner where memories dwell,
We weave our stories, weaving a spell.
With mismatched chairs and coffee stains galore,
Our laughter echoes; who could ask for more?

Cuddled up close with a book in hand,
We create our own whimsical wonderland.
With silly voices, we narrate the tale,
Our spirits dance happily, never to pale.

When snacks go missing, and we play the blame,
Our little café, it's still the same.
With crumb-filled laughter and tea-sipping cheer,
This haven we've built brings us closer each year.

So toast to our bond, forever unbroken,
With silliness fresh, and words left unspoken.
In this joyful hub, we'll always belong,
A haven where heartstrings sing their sweet song.

Under Starlit Canopies

Under a blanket of stars, we lie,
Tickling the clouds, and asking them why.
With silly wishes, we chuckle and sigh,
As fireflies dance, oh how they fly high!

A pizza slice on our wobbly plate,
We laugh at the cheese that won't quite stay straight.
With friendship as light in the night's embrace,
In this shared joy, we've found our right place.

Mismatched stories that twist and shout,
Finding our way, never in doubt.
With the moon as our lamp, shining so bright,
Together we wade through the sea of the night.

So raise up a glass to the fun that we share,
In this whimsical journey, we've not a care.
Under canopies woven from dreams overhead,
We giggle and chat, our hearts finely fed.

The Enclosure of Longing

In a fortress made of socks,
Where mismatched dreams reside,
I check for food and rocks,
My hopes are on a slide.

Walls of laughter, built with care,
Pillows project silly sighs,
A fortress of a teddy bear,
Where even giggles rise.

My heart's a trampoline of sorts,
Bouncing off the ceiling,
With every leap, it twists and torques,
To keep my joy revealing.

So if you hear a thumping sound,
It's just my heart at play,
In a castle spun of laughter,
Where silliness works all day.

Love's Safe Harbor

In a boat made out of fries,
We set sail on ketchup seas,
Navigating through the lies,
With a compass made of cheese.

The waves of giggles crash and roar,
While seagulls dance on deck,
We anchor dreams with silly lore,
With socks tied like a wreck.

Captain of the silly ship,
Check your heart's navigation,
With every snort and every quip,
We find humor's foundation.

So here's to love, our crazy art,
In this harbor, not so far,
With laughter's tides that never part,
You'll find where true joys are.

Beneath the Shelter of Dreams

Underneath a blanket fort,
Where stars can flip and twirl,
I tape my hopes of every sort,
While munching on a pearl.

The walls are made of whispered tales,
And popcorn hears our giggles,
As dreams drift in like tiny sails,
In a sea of joyful wiggles.

Here, we plot our cheeky schemes,
With crayons drawing fate,
In the land where nothing seems,
As silly as a cake.

So pull the covers, let's take flight,
On laughter's magical beam,
Beneath this shelter, pure delight,
We're floating on a dream.

Cocooned in Warmth

In a sofa made of marshmallows,
I curl and roll around,
Watching comedy of fellows,
With giggles as my sound.

Each cushion like a cloud so soft,
Hugs me tight like candy laces,
In this zone, I drift aloft,
With silly smiles on faces.

A blanket wrapped with smiles galore,
Like a hug that's never light,
Where laughter's worth a dozen score,
And every tickle's right.

So here I am, cocooned and free,
In warmth that feels like spring,
Each heartbeat sings a melody,
As joy takes flight on wing.

Beneath the Canvas of Affection

In a tent made of old socks,
We share our dreams and silly talks.
With laughter echoing through the seams,
Life's a circus, or so it seems.

Paint splatters on the floor,
We create art that's hard to ignore.
Spaghetti hanging from the beams,
Contraptions of absurd schemes.

Tickling fights over spilled juice,
Our love's a playful type of truce.
With a wink, we raise a toast,
To the chaos we cherish the most.

Underneath this wacky dome,
We've made a joyful little home.
Where laughter is the bright sun's spark,
In our fantastical, cozy park.

The Portrait of Shared Dreams

A canvas splashed with silly scenes,
Of all our quirks and daydreamed machines.
You painted me without a care,
In polka dots and crazy hair.

With each brushstroke, laughter swirls,
A masterpiece of twists and twirls.
Giggles captured on this frame,
In our wild, artistic game.

You pose too close, and I can't breathe,
Your tickles cause me to grieve.
Yet in this playful, vibrant mess,
Lies a heart that feels so blessed.

Each stroke a note in our song,
Where nothing silly feels too wrong.
Two artists in a world so bright,
Creating love's amusing light.

Mosaic of Love's Protection

Broken tiles, we make a floor,
Stumbling yet we laugh some more.
Each piece, a memory held tight,
In our patchwork's joyful sight.

Colorful shards from past debates,
Sticky notes and funny crates.
Our lives as mixed as jelly beans,
A quirky dance in life's routines.

Underneath this clumsy art,
We share a treasure, soul to heart.
No perfect patterns here combined,
Just mismatched joy, beautifully blind.

In every crack, there's laughter's glow,
Chasing silly dreams, we go.
In this mosaic, bright and true,
You and me, forever two.

In the Shadows of Shared Memories

In the corners where we hide,
Old jokes and laughter coincide.
With every whisper, stories swell,
Like secret fish tales we retell.

Worn-out shoes take center stage,
In our shared mischief, we engage.
Chasing moments that make us grin,
Finding joy in the mess within.

Our shadows dance, a happy crew,
Playing pranks, just me and you.
Pillow fights and snacks for two,
In this goofy rendezvous.

So let's create more silly schemes,
In the glow of shared dreams.
Where giggles thrive and laughter stays,
In our heart's whimsical maze.

www.ingramcontent.com/pod-product-compliance
Lightning Source LLC
Chambersburg PA
CBHW060115230426
43661CB00003B/198